The Best Contemporary Quilts

Quilt National
2001

The Best Contemporary Quilts
Quilt National
2001

Coproduced by **Lark Books & The Dairy Barn Cultural Arts Center**

LARK BOOKS

A Division of Sterling Publishing Co., Inc.
New York

Quilt National Project Director: **HILARY MORROW FLETCHER**

Editor: **KATHERINE DUNCAN AIMONE**

Art Director: **KATHLEEN J. HOLMES**

Photographer: **BRIAN BLAUSER**

Production Assistant: **HANNES CHAREN**

Additional photography provided by Seale Studios for Ann Adams (page 40), PRS Associates for B. J. Adams (page 96), Hester and Hardaway Photographers for Liz Axford (page 56), Peter Jenion for Elizabeth Brimelow (page 60), Pam Monfort for Jane Burch Cochran (page 101), J. Kevin Fitzsimmons for Nancy Crow (page 55), Caryl Bryer Fallert for her own work (page 18), David Caras for Beatriz Grayson (page 59), David Caras for Carol Anne Grotian (page 77), David Loveall Photography, Inc. for Wendy Huhn (page 100), John Bonath @ Moondog Studios for Debra Lunn and Michael Mrowka (page 73), Zohar Zaied for Linda MacDonald (page 90), DTT Studio for Patricia Malarcher (page 57), Luke Jordan for Eleanor McCain (page 14), Sam Newbury for Jan Myers-Newbury (page 48), David Belda Photography for Miriam Nathan-Roberts (page 95), Mary S. Renzy for Arturo Alonzo Sandoval (page 10), Karen Bell for Robin Schwalb (page 93), Anne Woringer for her own work (page 76).

Library of Congress Cataloging-in-Publication Data
Quilt National (2001 : Athens, Ohio)
    the best contemporary quilts : Quilt National 2001.
       p. cm.
    "Coproduced by Lark Books and The Dairy Barn Cultural Arts Center."
    Includes bibliographical references.
    ISBN 1-57990-217-0
    1. Quilts—United States—History—20th century—Exhibitions.   2. Quilts—History—
      20th century—Exhibitions. I. Lark Books. II. Dairy Barn Southeastern Ohio
      Cultural Arts Center.   III. Title.
  NK9112.Q5 20001
  746.46'0973'07477197—dc21   2001016485
                                        CIP

10 9 8 7 6 5 4 3 2

Published by Lark Books, a division of
Sterling Publishing Co., Inc.
387 Park Avenue South, New York, N.Y. 10016

Distributed in Canada by Sterling Publishing,
c/o Canadian Manda Group, One Atlantic Ave., Suite 105
Toronto, Ontario, Canada M6K 3E7

Distributed in the U.K. by Guild of Master Craftsman Publications Ltd., Castle Place
166 High Street, Lewes, East Sussex, England BN7 1XU
Tel: (+ 44) 1273 477374, Fax: (+ 44) 1273 478606, Email: pubs@thegmcgroup.com
Web: www.gmcpublications.com

Distributed in Australia by Capricorn Link (Australia) Pty Ltd.,
P.O. Box 704, Windsor, NSW 2756, Australia

If you have questions or comments about this book, please contact:
Lark Books, 67 Broadway, Asheville, NC 28801, (828) 236-9730

Printed in China.

ISBN 1-57990-217-0

On the cover, a detail of *Feather Study #14* by Caryl Bryer Fallert
On page 1, Rosemary Hoffenberg
Opposite page from left to right, details of quilts by Marie Wohadlo, Kanti Jocelyn, Noël M. Ruessmann and Denise Burge
On page 11 from left to right, details of quilts by Libby Lehman, Harue Konishi, Jane Lloyd, Sue Benner and Pat Kroth

CONTENTS

FOREWORD

THIS BOOK PRESENTS THE WORK of the 12th Quilt National biennial exhibition presented by the Dairy Barn Southeastern Ohio Cultural Arts Center in Athens, Ohio. The show continues to present the newest and best work by contemporary quilt artists to more than 7,000 Dairy Barn visitors as well as an estimated 30,000 visitors at galleries and museums during its two-year tour. The high quality of the work and the artistic vision of the artists have kept the show vital since its birth 22 years ago. We hope for the show's success to continue well into the 21st century.

Quilt National '01 was juried from slides by three outstanding figures in the world of fiber art who reviewed more than 1,411 entries by approximately 670 artists from around the United States and abroad. We thank these jurors for their hard work and dedication to great choices: Melissa Leventon, Curator of Textiles, Fine Art Museums of San Francisco; fiber artist Arturo Alonzo Sandoval; and quilt artist Jane A. Sassaman.

This beautiful publication is the result of the talent and vision of several people at Lark Books. We are grateful for the help of the Director of Publishing, Carol Taylor; Editor, Katherine Duncan Aimone; and Art Director, Kathleen Holmes.

A show of this magnitude requires the investment of time and talents as well as money. We thank all of our sponsors for their continued funding. We are fortunate to have the major support of the Fairfield Processing Corporation, makers of Poly-fil products. Additional funding comes from Mr. Tadanobu Seto and *Quilts Japan* magazine; Friends of Fiber Art International; the James Foundation; Studio Art Quilt Associates; the Ohio Arts Council; Ohio University Inn; *The Athens Messenger*; Larry Conrath Realty; the city of Athens; the family of Lynn Goodwin Borgman; and Ginko Studio & Gallery (Oberlin, Ohio).

We are grateful to Hilary Morrow Fletcher, Quilt National Project Director for the past 18 years, for her unflinching commitment to the quilt world. We also express appreciation and thanks to our exhibition designer, Ann Moneypenny, and photographer, Brian Blauser.

For more than 20 years, Quilt National has set standards and served as a model for other art quilt shows. Please visit our beautiful facility at the Dairy Barn to see this stunning show in its entirety as well as our year-long schedule of changing fine art and craft exhibitions.

Susan Cole Urano
Executive Director

THIS IS THE FIRST QUILT NATIONAL of the 21st century. As we travel the path to the future, it seems like a good time to consider where we have been, where we are now, and where this path might take us in the years to come.

The history of the medium of layered and stitched fabric tells us that the 1970s saw a resurgence of interest in the beauty of one-of-a-kind handmade objects as opposed to the blandness and uniformity of mass market manufactured goods. Most of the quilt books and magazines published at the time sought to teach an ever-widening audience how to make classic pieced and/or appliquéd bedcovers.

The 1970s were also a time when there was neither understanding of nor tolerance for works that deviated from the accepted norms. This was the environment in which Nancy Crow and a handful of other artists found themselves. The purpose of the first Quilt National in 1979 was to provide an exhibit opportunity to artists whose work was unwelcome by the organizers of the existing quilt shows.

I know from firsthand experience that some visitors to the early Quilt National exhibitions never really "saw" the quilts. They were too busy commenting on the facts that the quilts were not what they expected and that they were, in the opinion of some, not what they should be. Other visitors were people like me who, once exposed to Quilt National, quickly realized that quilts could be something other than functional objects.

There were also people, many of whom are represented in this book, who were inspired and emboldened by what they saw. They looked at works by Nancy Halpern, Michael James, and the other pioneers of the art quilt movement and recognized that this medium would enable them to make artistic statements that simply could not be made with other materials. That was where we were.

And where are we now? In the 22 years since Quilt National began, the making of both functional and nonfunctional quilts has become a worldwide activity. There are quilters' organizations, publications, and exhibitions on nearly every continent. Artists from 24 countries (including the United States) submitted works for consideration by the Quilt National '01 jurors. Nearly one-quarter of the entries were accompanied by forms that had been downloaded from the Quilt National Internet site, and 69 percent of those were from people who had no previous direct contact with the Dairy Barn and Quilt National.

With the pervasiveness of the Internet, a fiber artist in Denmark can communicate with one from New Zealand as easily as two quiltmakers living on the same street. Information about new techniques and materials is disseminated quickly through online discussion groups, resource pages, and individual Web sites. Shopping in cyberspace gives even the most remote quiltmaker access to nearly all of the raw materials that are available to artists who live in a modern "megalopolis."

INTRODUCTION

Now both quiltmakers and nonquiltmakers are beginning to understand that there is absolutely no difference between what today's quiltmakers are doing and what our great-grandmothers did decades ago: They are using currently available materials and techniques to express their individual creativity and to make tangible, long-lasting statements about themselves and their world.

Unfortunately, there are millions of people who remain unaware of the wonder and the diversity of today's quilts. They have not yet been exposed to works that are "quilts" by virtue of their structure rather than their function.

And what about 20 years from now, where will we be? That, of course, is the million-dollar question, and there are many more than four answer options. My hope is that a significant percentage of the nonquilting world will recognize that "quilt" is not a monolithic concept. They will see exhibitions like Quilt National, or they will be exposed to images of innovative quilts in newspapers, magazines, books, and on the Internet. Perhaps they will be like my now two-year-old granddaughter who will have grown up with quilts on her walls. Through these experiences, they will gain an appreciation for all expressions of this art form.

My most fervent hope is that the nonquilting world will no longer be surprised at the variety of objects that are identified as quilts. Most important, people will recognize that the concepts of "quilt" and "art" are NOT incompatible.

And what about the quiltmakers? What will they be doing 20 years from now? That question is easy! The answer can be found back when it all started. With all the wisdom of Nostradamus, Beth Gutcheon ends the introduction to her 1973 book, *The Perfect Patchwork Primer*, with the following words: "Modern quiltmakers are bringing their craft to a new maturity, reflecting their spirits and their times, and there is even reason to expect that some of the best of the tradition is yet to come."

Hilary Morrow Fletcher
Quilt National Project Director

JURORS' STATEMENTS

JANE A. SASSAMAN
Chicago, Illinois

From its inception in 1979, Quilt National strove to be the definitive showcase for innovative contemporary art quilts. Today, more than 20 years later, acceptance into this international competition and exhibition continues to be the ultimate aspiration for many quilters.

In the early eighties when I was beginning my career as an art quilter, my loftiest goal was to have my work accepted into a Quilt National competition. When I accepted the invitation to help select the pieces for Quilt National '01, I knew the importance of the assignment because of my own experience. I was also delighted to be able to share the responsibility with two experienced colleagues—Arturo Sandoval and Melissa Leventon.

As jurors, we were informed ahead of time that we had more than 1,400 entries to view and could select only 85 to 90 pieces for the show—a seemingly overwhelming chore. As we strode toward the Dairy Barn on a gray morning to take on this task, I imagined us as three undercover agents assigned to an important mission. Thanks to Hilary and her crew, this difficult job went smoothly. The Dairy Barn's well-practiced organization of the process made it efficient and pleasant.

The first viewing of slides presented us with an interesting overview— one so vast that it contained works by everyone from Sunday quilters to the Picassos of the field. Almost half the quilts were sorted out during the next round, and slides that were unmasked, poorly lit, and out of focus were eliminated.

With each successive round of scoring, the number of finalists grew smaller. Because only one quilt per artist could be accepted, we viewed multiple entries together and picked the best representative piece for the show. Individual pieces shown in the context of a consistent body of work appeared stronger, and it was apparent that these individuals had evolved their own artistic languages. By comparison, if each quilt submitted by an individual differed wildly from the others, we were inclined to assume that the work was derivative.

Finally, we agreed upon the strength of 200 quilts. Each was worthy of attention, and we would have been satisfied to stop there. For this reason, the next round of jurying was the most difficult. We discussed and compromised, balanced and weighed, until we made our final choices for a show of diverse and extraordinary art

Metamorphosis is about transformation and potential. A seed gestates in the muddy underworld and explodes toward the sun—an obvious metaphor for human life, discovery, and the development of innate potential.

JANE A. SASSAMAN, *Metamorphosis*

Cotton fabrics; machine appliquéd and machine quilted; 29 by 78 inches (72.5 by 195 cm).

quilts. I had anticipated more disagreements among us, but the strongest quilts separated themselves naturally from the others. We reviewed each of the 1,411 slides one more time before viewing all of them together as a show. At this point, we relied on Melissa's keen curatorial eye to make sure that the selection of works would make a coherent exhibition.

During the jurying process, I was overwhelmed by the passion of the art quilt movement. Willing to spend countless hours in solitary communion with his or her materials, the art quilter's close relationship with the medium of quilting often overpowers other considerations. Such passion infuses the works that you see in this exhibition with energy and a joyous affirmation of individuality. These artists are proof that instant gratification is not a goal for everyone in contemporary society. In fact, I believe that quilting is an act of quiet rebellion—a reminder that some of us are still willing to pursue work that requires a slower, more contemplative pace. I am proud to be a part of a movement made up of such independent and devoted people.

After graduating from Iowa State University, where she studied textile and jewelry design, **Jane A. Sassaman** worked as a window dresser, illustrator, and a designer of decorative accessories while actively searching for just the right medium through which she could express her creative energies. When she discovered art quilts in 1980, she knew that her search was over. During the course of her 20-year career, she has developed a distinctive style and is frequently invited to teach and share her knowledge and skills with countless enthusiastic students. Her work has been included in many prestigious exhibitions, including six previous Quilt National exhibitions.

MELISSA LEVENTON

San Francisco, California

The task of an exhibition jury is to create a coherent exhibition from the available entries. In the case of Quilt National '01, the necessity of selecting fewer than 90 quilts from a pool of more than 1,400 submissions was both a serious responsibility and an exhilarating challenge. Sitting in a darkened room and peering at bright, shifting images of quilts is an exercise that underscores the many different ways of seeing and evaluating art. Each quilt always appears a little differently in each subsequent round of viewing, while our necessary choices narrowed the pool. I am proud of our final selections, but regretful that there were many more fine and worthy quilts than we had space to include.

As a curator and nonquiltmaker, I brought a slightly different perspective to the jury. Like most curators, I try to keep the big picture in mind when choosing objects for an exhibition so that the resulting show is full of works that are not only wonderful in themselves but make sense together. In the quest to construct a cohesive Quilt National exhibition, I looked for visual harmonies and thematic or technical correspondences that would complement each other visually or serve to illustrate specific ideas or trends. I saw much that was exciting in this year's 1,411 submissions. Quilts lend themselves to bold graphic statements, and many of the submissions were confidently and stunningly beautiful. For example, our Award of Excellence winner, *Floating 1* by Ruth Garrison, is a marvelous combination of color and pattern in various picture planes.

Revisiting Jackson is a very different kind of tour de force—an amazingly successful evocation of a Jackson Pollock painting that also functions as a sly commentary on the continued (and, to my mind, regrettable) dominance of painting in the art world pantheon. I respond to artworks that carry cultural or political messages as well as those that are humorous. *Heroic Optimism* (the Domini McCarthy Award winner) is a good example of the former and *Corporate Attire* (the Emerging Artist Award winner) of the latter. *Corporate Attire* also appeals to me because of its reference to traditional quilts.

One of my desires as a curator and collector is to promote and encourage artists to connect their contemporary textile creations with textile traditions, and I looked particularly for those sorts of connections in the competition entries. For this reason, I selected *Workman's Quilt* for my Juror's Award of Merit. Though newly created, it strongly and appealingly referenced the workaday quilts of an earlier era.

This connection also influenced the jury's choice for Best of Show: the beautiful, hand-quilted *Autumn Leaves Triptych*. This piece, in which quilting takes center stage, is thoroughly modern—though with an enticing stillness and intimacy that are a rare and compelling bridge to quilts past.

Melissa Leventon's educational history includes an undergraduate degree from Brandeis University (Waltham, Massachusetts) and a master's degree from Courtauld Institute of Art, University of London (England). She is the author of several publications, including a forthcoming book, *Art on Your Sleeve: A History of Art to Wear.* Ms. Leventon has been affiliated with The Fine Arts Museums of San Francisco since 1986, and now serves as Curator of Textiles.

ARTURO ALONZO SANDOVAL
Lexington, Kentucky

Creativity and diversity reigned among the more than 1,400 slides submitted by 670 artists for Quilt National '01. Viewing so many wonderful works assured me that the field of art quilting is very much alive and well.

This show had more entries than any other for which I've served as a juror, and the task of selecting the final selections from so many fine works was truly daunting. The charge to pare the slides down from 1,411 to between 85 and 90 seemed absurd at first. Nevertheless, the task was amicably shared with my co-jurors, Melissa Leventon and Jane Sassaman, who brought understanding of the nuances of textiles and art quilts to the table. The staff and volunteer crew at the Dairy Barn, headed by Hilary Morrow Fletcher, made the task manageable, timely, and pleasant during the two days that we spent together.

My viewpoint for making selections is always supported by my bias as an art educator in fine arts and crafts, and I was able to comfortably infuse the process with this knowledge. Decisions were made after periods of discussion and multiple viewings of the slides. Entries that we felt were derivative were not considered after we decided that such works were obvious spin-offs of other ideas. Instead, we searched for the personal voice in entries employing unusual designs, ideas, and materials. As with any co-jurying process, not all of the works I was passionate about made the final rounds.

Looking at the entries as a whole, I was impressed by the high quality of the ideas and the craftsmanship of the works. About 90 percent of the entry images were well-documented in the slides. Slides that were too dark or those showing backgrounds (such as people or furniture) lost their chance of being considered. If artists hope for their work to be considered in any juried competion, they must submit professional, quality slides—these slides serve as the only view of the work that the juror has. It's my hope that all of our selections make the quilt specifications listed in the slide prospectus after they arrive at the Dairy Barn. It would be a travesty to have any of the selections that we've chosen be eliminated.

Finally, for my Juror's Choice Award I selected a quilt by B. J. Adams, *A Seasonal Spectrum*, which caught my eye with its use of a personal and skillful technique creating dimensional embroidery, representation, and three-dimensional illusion.

Arturo Alonzo Sandoval received his basic art training at California State College in Los Angeles. Following a stint in the U.S. Navy during the Vietnam War, he entered graduate school at Cranbrook Academy of Art in Michigan. He has held teaching positions at Southern Illinois University at Edwardsville and at the University of Kentucky, where he is now a tenured professor of art. His resume includes an impressive and extensive list of solo and group exhibitions as well as awards. His works are included in several important collections, including the Museum of Modern Art (New York, New York); Skidmore, Owings and Merrill (Houston, Texas); and the Waverly Hotel (Atlanta, Georgia).

ARTURO ALONZO SANDOVAL,
Millennium Portal No. 3

Various materials including mylar, plastic, paint, netting, colored threads, canvas, polymer medium, and nonwoven interfacing; interlaced and machine appliquéd, embroidered and stitched; 72 inches (182.9 cm) in diameter.

My process begins with discoveries from my collected pile of recycled canvases painted by students. Working in a direct appliqué method, I use circular pieces of canvas as dominant forces in the compositions. My ideas for the pieces are designed to relate to the biblical statement: "My father's house has many mansions." I proceed by developing atmospheric and spatial elements for the background with netting, transparent fabrics, and machine embroidery. The use of mylar as a design element incorporates my interest in the use of kinetic elements with reflective surfaces. The pieces are backed with cotton fabrics adhered with polymer medium. The edges are finished off using machine stitching.

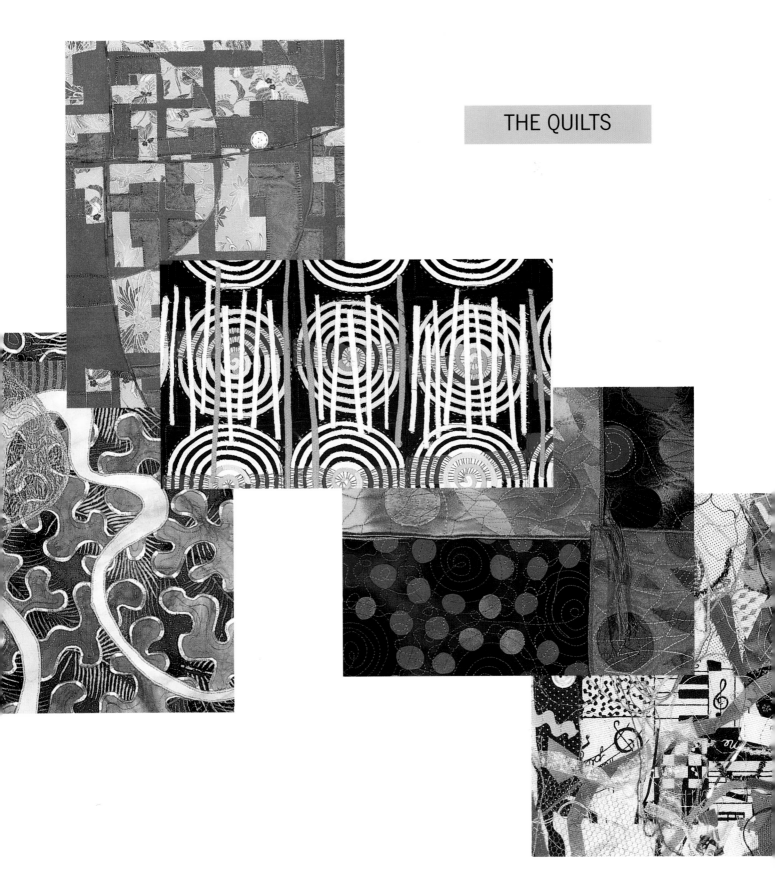

THE QUILTS

Atlantis
Commercial and hand-dyed
cotton fabrics; machine
pieced and machine
quilted; 59 by 59 inches
(149.9 by 149.9 cm).

The legend of Atlantis maintains that this fictional island once existed before sinking into the Atlantic Ocean. We all dream

Ruth Eissfeldt
Essen, Germany

about someday discovering a beautiful island or a lost paradise. I, too, am always looking for my private Atlantis, and it is an ardent desire that will never be fulfilled.

Pond Life
Hand-dyed cotton broad-
cloth; improvisationally
pieced and machine
quilted; 56 by 35 inches
(142.3 by 88.9 cm).

Color and abstract forms are what drive my work. The inspiration for this work was a beautiful piece of hand-dyed fabric with areas that

Virginia Abrams
Hockessin, Delaware

appeared to glow with light. In the background of the piece, I built up various levels of greens (representing plants) and blues (representing water currents) to give depth to the work. In the foreground, I added bright yellow greens and fuchsia to give the feeling of springtime.

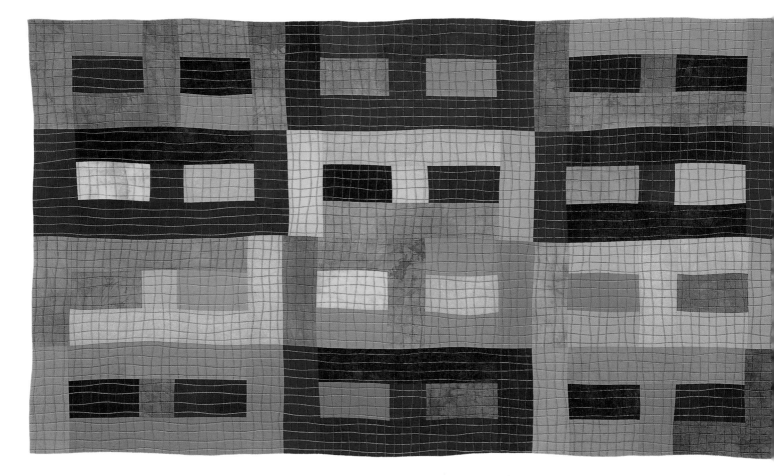

Blue/Green/Yellow Rectangles
Cotton fabrics, hand dyed by the artist and by others; machine pieced and quilted; 106 by 60 inches (269.2 by 152.4 cm).

I am interested in the interaction of color, shape, and line. This quilt is a three-color study of object/ground relation-

Eleanor A. McCain
Shalimar, Florida

ships. The overlay of the quilt grid and its interplay with color shapes are the focus of this exploration.

Via Matt Fields
Hand-painted and hand-dyed cotton fabric; machine pieced and embroidered, hand quilted; 55 by 60 inches (139.7 by 152.4 cm).

Matt Fields is a place to stop and lean your elbows

Anne Smith
Warrington, Cheshire, England

on the gate, to listen and take stock, and perhaps find a different route to the place you think you want to go—before moving on.

BEST OF SHOW

Autumn Leaves Triptych

Silk and linen fabrics; hand quilted and hand embellished with painted cotton and linen leaves; 61 by 76 inches (154.9 by 193 cm).

It is late autumn at dusk. Here and there an individual leaf captures the day's final slanting light and is briefly illuminated. The burnished gold is contrasted by the deep purple of the shadows. The oriental influence in my work is apparent—the three hanging panels are meant to suggest a kimono.

Noël M. Ruessmann
Stroudsburg, Pennsylvania

**Reisefieber
(Anticipating the
Journey)**
Hand-dyed and commercial
cottons; machine pieced and
machine quilted; 44 by 65
inches (111.8 by 165.1 cm).

This quilt is part of a series called *Journeys* that is
about journeys of exploration. Investigating the motif-
driven design in
this piece is also
a part of this exploration.

Jutta Farringer
Capetown, South Africa

Feather Study #14
Hand-dyed and hand-painted
cotton fabrics; machine
pieced and machine quilted;
56 by 56 inches (142.3 by
142.3 cm).

This quilt is one of a series inspired by a close-up of a fantasy feather
that evolved from a series of hundreds of drawings on this theme.

Caryl Bryer Fallert
Oswego, Illinois

The illusion of light in this quilt
was created by using fabric
dyed in gradations of color and value. These gradations intersect in
the plumes of the feathers to create areas of emerging and
submerging contrast and luminosity.

Movement #6
Cotton and silk fabrics
(some of which have
been painted); machine
pieced and machine
quilted; 75 by 75 inches
(190.5 by 190.5 cm).

The petals, opening timidly from the bud, are gradually blossoming into a big flower. Breathing in the fresh air under the brilliant

Yasuko Saito
Tokyo, Japan

sunlight, the newly born flower is gaining its vivid color and, at last, showing us its energy—its will to live.

19

My recent work is about the distortion of light. This piece is inspired by the idea of light refracted through a prism that generates alternating colors and

Tim Harding
Stillwater, Minnesota

patterns. I wanted to create a somewhat transparent hanging that could be viewed from both sides to create depth and patterning shifts as the viewer moves. This piece has a transient dynamic similar to the dappled patterns of sunlight penetrating the leafy canopy of a forest.

Prism Quilt
Manipulated layers of silk with reverse appliqué process cut through quilted layers to reveal others behind the surface (including a sheer silk organza sublayer); front and back hung between spacer bars to allow an open air layer and sheer sublayers to be randomly visible throughout; 60 by 71 inches (152.4 by 180.3 cm). (Front view on page 20, reverse view on page 21.)

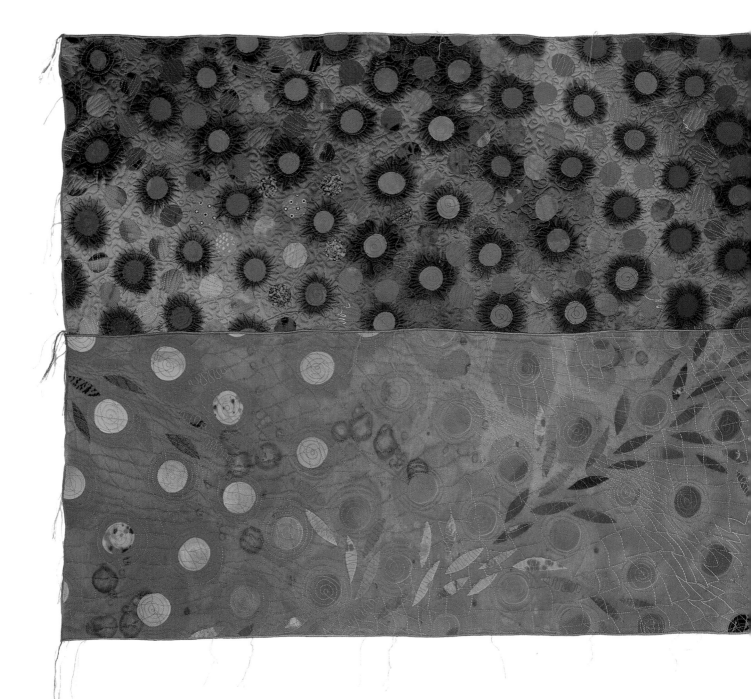

Skin Deep II continues my exploration of watery environments with musings about the skins of imagined fish, amphibians, and other mysterious creatures. A quilt can be a covering, and a quilt can have a type of skin.

Sue Benner
Dallas, Texas

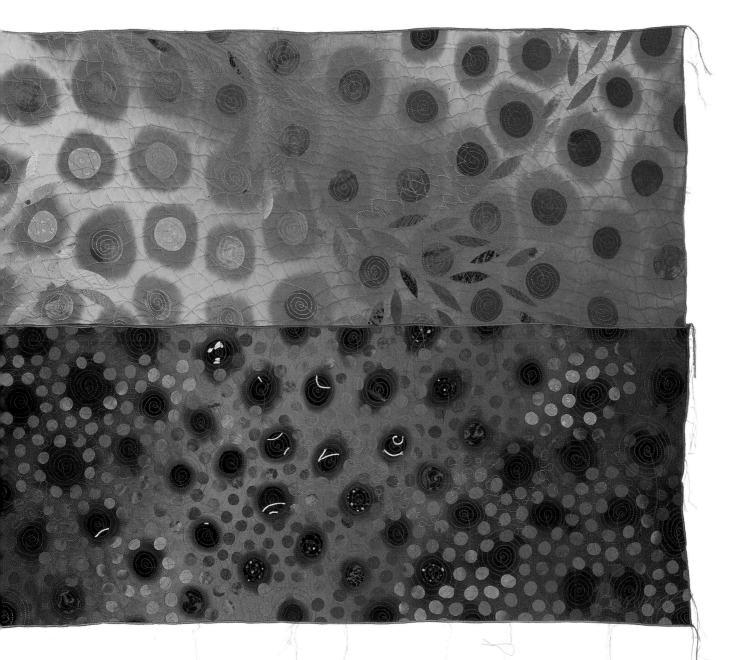

Skin Deep II
Commercial and hand-dyed
silk and polyester fabrics;
fused and machine quilted;
83 by 34 inches (210.8 by
86.4 cm).

Calligraphy I
Cotton fabric painted with
fiber-reactive dyes;
machine pieced and
quilted; 54 by 32 inches
(137.1 by 81.3 cm).

The force of the calligraphic mark, the trace of the individual gesture holding the movement, and the energy of the hand fascinate me. In this piece I have intuitively extended and cropped the gesture, focusing its energy in a terse statement. This quilt is the first in an ongoing series centered on the power of calligraphy as a personal mark.

Angela Moll
Santa Barbara, California

Short Poppies Are Valuable Too
Hand-dyed and commercial silk, lamé and blended fabrics; direct appliqué with fusing and stitches, machine quilted; 39 by 54 inches (99.1 by 137.2 cm).

This work was made in response to a movement in Australia known as "Refabricating the Future." It offers an alternative to the present in which short and tall poppies work together harmoniously to produce a nurturing, caring, valued, and productive future for all.

Alison Muir
Sydney, Australia

Life Force
Torn fabrics, stitched in
layers to canvas; machine
stitched and machine
quilted; 57 by 54 inches
(144.8 by 137.2 cm.)

The combination of yellows and reds always excites me. They

Judy Hooworth
Sydney, Australia

are the colors of life—

energy and passion, fire

and blood, cheese and tomatoes, happiness and sin, butter-

cups and roses, illumination and atonement, bananas and

apples, sunshine and sunsets....

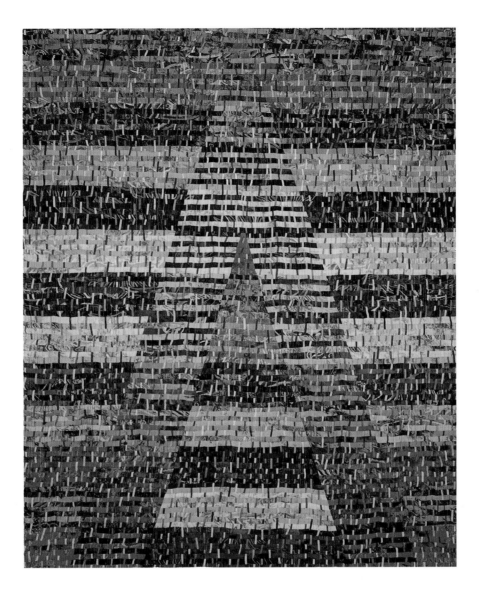

Celebration
Commercial rayon fabric that has been hand painted, stitched to the foundation, and woven with hand-painted strips of silk ribbon; machine quilted; 41 by 51 inches (104.1 by 129.5 cm).

Prior to creating quilts, I was a weaver. I'm still fascinated by this process and wanted to cre-

Kanti Jocelyn
Kanagawa, Japan

ate the illusion of woven cloth in this quilt. The triangle is a symbol of the triune nature of existence—a celebration of life.

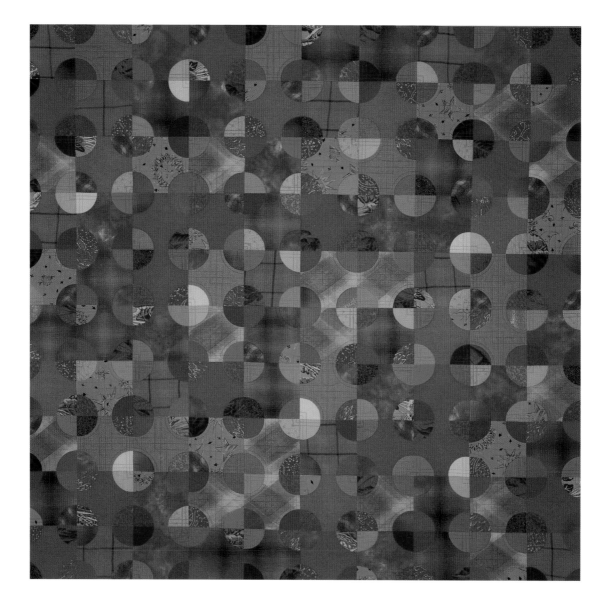

Full Circle
Commercial cottons;
machine pieced and
machine quilted; 80 by
80 inches (203.2 by
203.2 cm). On loan
from a private collection.

I was spurred to undertake an immersion in red through a friend's
commission for a quilt. This quilt is about color, repetition,
contrast, and playing my
intuition against the basic
geometric structure of a good old traditional quilt design. Even
though it is nonobjective and abstract, it is full of personal history,
symbolism, and emotional experience.

Rebecca Rohrkaste
Berkeley, California

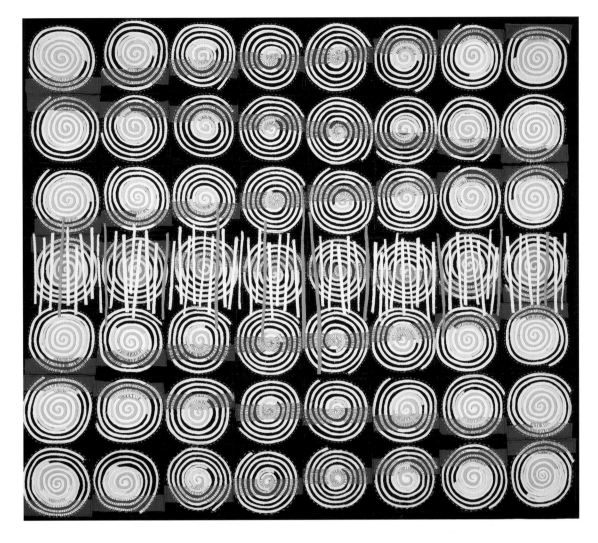

Spiral Shock
Cottons and blends;
machine pieced, hand
and machine embroidered;
37 by 33 inches (94 by
83.8 cm).

The spiral is a simple shape that evokes the past and

appears on ancient stones near my home. I am totally

Jane Lloyd absorbed and fasci-
Ballymena, County Antrim,
Northern Ireland nated by this shape

on the stones. This is one of a series of spiral

quilts that I'm making.

FG Block AB
Hand-printed and dyed fabrics; machine pieced and quilted; 60 by 75 inches (152.4 by 190.5 cm).

This piece was inspired by the long study of a concrete block. My design process begins with computer drawings that allow me to experiment with many different colors and layering possibilities, but these images are quite different from the results I achieve with silk screens, fabrics, and inks. FG stands for "flying geese," which refers to the repeated triangles. AB stands for "Ari's bed," because I originally intended this quilt for my son Ari's bed.

Ellen Oppenheimer
Oakland, California

Pennsylvania 6-5000, Please
100 percent cotton fabric; machine pieced and machine quilted; 56 by 63 inches (142.2 by 160 cm).

This piece is the first of a series that involves a block with an unusual shape. The angles were difficult to calculate, and I was pleased when all of the pieces fit together.

Sharon Heidingsfelder
Little Rock, Arkansas

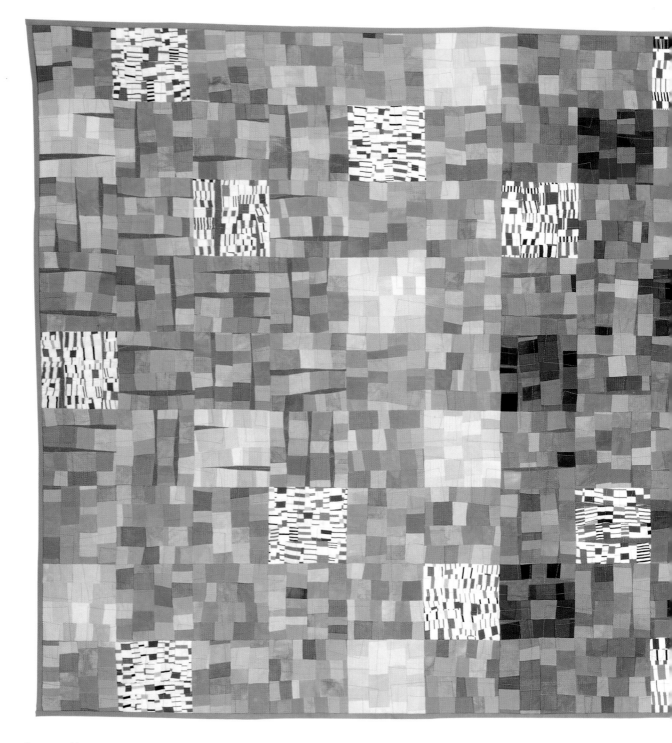

AWARD OF EXCELLENCE

Two sets of strip-pieced fabrics that are different in character are brought together in this piece. The high contrast allows the frenzied strips to float above a calm sea of blue-green solids.

Ruth Garrison
Tempe, Arizona

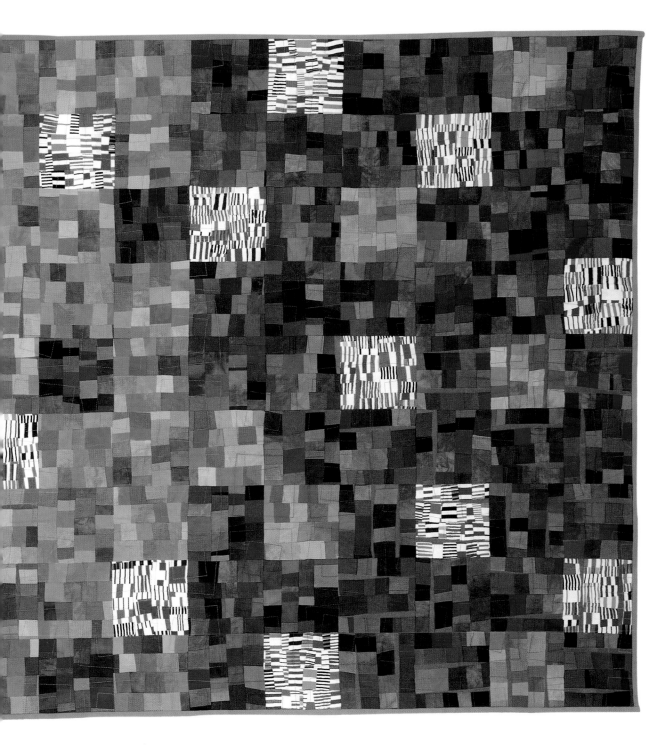

Floating I
Cotton fabrics (some hand
dyed and screen printed);
machine pieced and machine
quilted; 83 by 41 inches
(210.8 by 104.1 cm).

Solar Energy
Commercial and hand-dyed cottons; machine pieced, hand appliquéd and machine quilted; 41 by 41 inches (104.1 by 104.1 cm).

Quilting is essentially a two-dimensional medium. My goal is to add the third dimension. I want the viewer to look into my pieces and feel

Colleen Wise
Puyallup, Washington

detached, floating, slightly disoriented, and disconnected from gravity. *Solar Energy* is one piece in a series involving celestial events. Enjoy your little trip into space!

Falling
Cotton fabrics; hand
appliquéd through all
layers; 46 by 68
inches (116.8 by
172.7 cm).

This piece was inspired by Paul Gauguin's painting titled *The Flageolet Player on the Cliff.*
My goal was to abstract the dynamic lines in the painting, which converge and then fall.

Anne McKenzie Nickolson
Indianapolis, Indiana

The layering of stripes, the grid
structure, and the color con-
trasts create a system of tensions that add to the complexity of the work and the feeling
of movement. The production of this piece was assisted by the Indiana Arts Commission
and the National Endowment for the Arts.

Vibrations from the striking of a gong move outward in repeating patterns—just as my creative decisions for one quilt affect my future work. In a similar way, the

Carol Taylor
Pittsford, New York

vibrations in this piece emanate from the lightest areas and echo outward with darkening values and diminishing sizes. Each quarter circle motif is an original—individually cut and pieced—with four combined into a fractured gong. A square framework contains each gong; similarly, I contain or limit the challenges I assign myself. Free-motion quilted circles heighten the illusion of resonating tones throughout the quilt.

Vibrations
Hand-dyed cotton sateen fabrics by Heide Stoll-Weber, Judy Robertson, Regina Goodman, and the artist; improvisationally cut, machine pieced, and free-motion machine quilted; 56 by 67 inches (142.2 by 170.2 cm).

Tropic of Cancer
Multiple layers of acrylic-painted silk organza on top of a quilted cotton and linen base; machine pieced and quilted; 48 by 60 inches (121.9 by 152.4 cm).

This quilt is the third in a series that emphasizes line and pattern, but also the uniqueness of the quilt medium. The seam lines provide a strong design element, while

Nelda Warkentin
Anchorage, Alaska

multiple layers of transparent silk give the work depth and add a painterly quality. Multicolored, free-form quilt stitches add interest and movement.

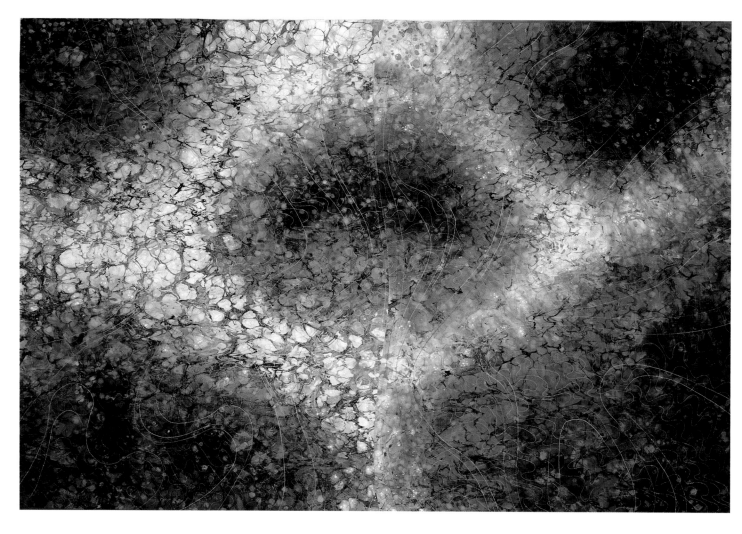

Wind and Wave III
Dye-painted cotton sateen
which has been discharged,
spattered, and monotyped
with textile paints; free-
motion machine quilting with
hand-dyed silk, cotton and
rayon threads; 76 by 50
inches (193.1 by 127 cm).

Patterns of light and air flowing across water

echo patterns of emotions flowing across life.

Sharon Meares Commins
Los Angeles, California

Cloud Forest
Silk fabric embellished with acrylic paint and embroidery; hand appliquéd and hand stitched; 56 by 42 inches (142.2 by 106.7 cm).

When I look at a scene in nature, I watch the changes going on around me—the visual elements, their movement, the light that

Emily Richardson
Philadelphia, Pennsylvania

defines them, and the atmosphere that surrounds them. These changes, along with my own shifting point of view, lead to the components of my work. In *Cloud Forest*, I used layers of painted sheer fabrics to evoke this shifting sense of a place where the trees and the sky have an exchange.

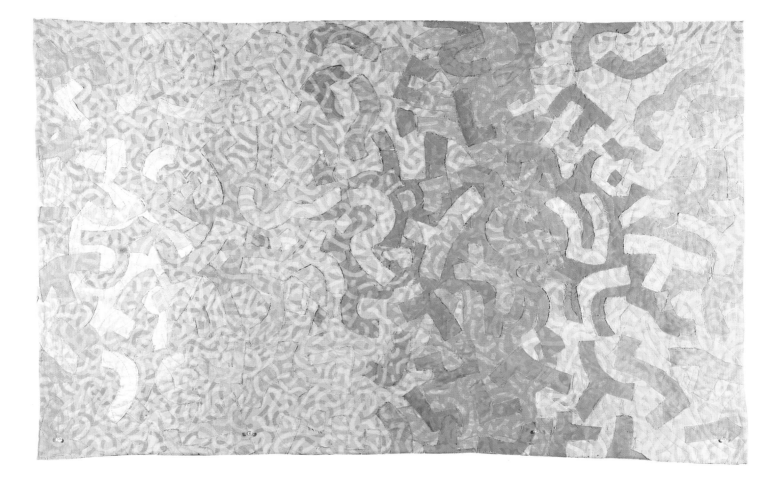

**Chroma Zones VII:
Kuba Chroma**
Silk and linen fabrics that
have been hand dyed, silk
screened, and discharged;
machine pieced and
appliquéd, machine quilted;
53 by 32 inches (134.6 by
80 cm).

My *Chroma Zone* quilt series is based on a block that includes 10 geometric shapes that have been modified by substituting curves for

Ann M. Adams
San Antonio, Texas

right angles. The resulting curved templates are very similar to shapes found in African textiles from the Kuba Kingdom in Zaire. They seem to convey a message and suggest living things. The fabric is mottled with printed calligraphic forms that appear to relate to the figures. Through this series I am experimenting with figure-ground relationships and illusions as well as an expanded palette.

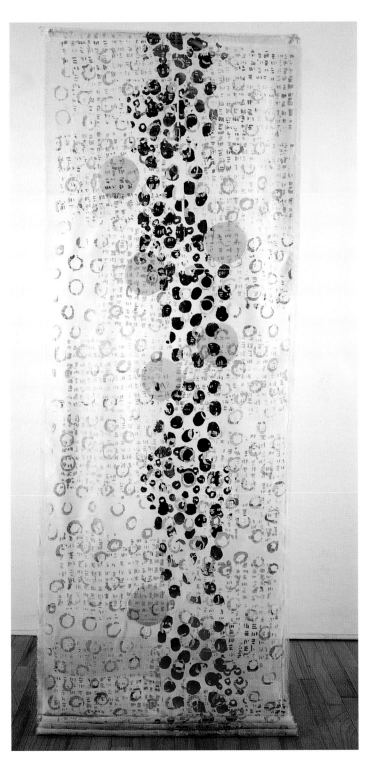

Meditation Seven
Cotton batting and sheer polyester fabric that has been patterned with screen printing textile paint as well as laminated newspaper and gold leafing; hand quilted; 28 by 108 inches (71.1 by 274.3 cm) as installed.

I continue to explore the visual surface as a means of investigating spirituality. This piece alludes to the seven chakras and was inspired by the contemplation of my energetic being—my physical self as it relates to my mental self. When I challenge myself to move beyond what I've already done and know, the physical and the mental combine in exhilarating and surprising ways.

Jane Dunnewold
San Antonio, Texas

The tall grasses in the shallow areas of the northwestern Wisconsin

lakes are so peaceful and beautiful. These areas continue to inspire

Connie Scheele
Houston, Texas

my work. To emphasize the

height of the grasses, I made

the quilt long horizontally and short vertically.

Where the Grass Grows Tall
Hand-dyed cottons; machine pieced and hand quilted with silk threads; 83 by 37 inches (210.8 by 94 cm). On loan from a private collection.

Tempest
100 percent black Thai silk that has been hand patterned with discharged dye and a variety of Japanese arashi shibori techniques; machine pieced and machine quilted; 52 by 87 inches (132.1 by 221 cm).

I think of my work as abstract interpretations of stone, sky, fire, and water. My current work is inspired by the windswept, fog-enveloped Northern California coastal marshes. I am fasci-

Judith Content
Palo Alto, California

nated by the play of light and shadow as the fog descends or dissipates in the sunlight. *Tempest* was inspired by the winds and waves of storms that sweep in across the Pacific in winter, obscured by fog until they're upon you.

Too Close to Home
Cotton fabrics hand painted and patterned by the artist through a variety of techniques, including stenciling, typography, and offset typesetting; machine pieced, appliquéd, embroidered, and quilted; 60 by 65 inches (152.4 by 165.1cm).

My work comes from feelings within. Examining them closely, these feelings find form, meaning, and sometimes resolution within the work. A comment, a poem, and a personal relationship were the inspiration/catalyst for this piece.

Lonni Rossi
Wynnewood, Pennsylvania

Ground Cloth
Rust print on cotton fabrics with overprinting, dyeing, and discharging techniques; machine pieced and quilted; 72 by 50 inches (182.9 by 127 cm).

The surface qualities of aged and weathered materials intrigue me—such as the rust stain left from a nail in exposed wood or layers of chipped and crackled paint on an old chair. In *Ground Cloth* I have created patterns and marks by

Laura Conners
Crawfordsville, Indiana

exposing fabric to rusted metal surfaces before using overprinting, dyeing, and discharging techniques to build up rich surfaces. The imagery on these fabrics can be unpredictable, and the random nature of this working style requires an intuitive approach and an innovative response. The work reflects a kind of spontaneity and freshness that are uniquely my own.

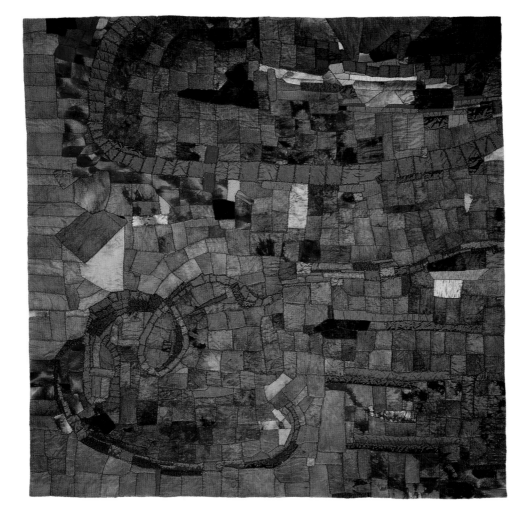

Visible Solitude
Silk fabric (hand dyed by
Renee B. Gentz), hand
appliquéd to muslin, hand
embroidered and embel-
lished with glass beads;
hand quilted; 65 by 65
inches (165.1 by 165.1 cm).

I walk along the Erie Canal every morning. The changing

Mary Ann Scarborough
Holley, New York

light, reflections,

and colors are a

daily lesson in combinations and possibilities.

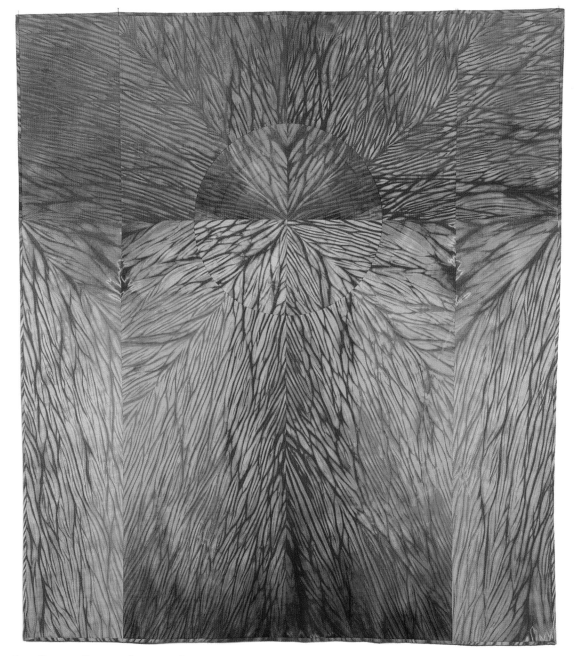

LYNN GOODWIN BORGMAN AWARD FOR SURFACE DESIGN

Icarus
Cotton muslin fabric hand dyed using arashi shibori technique; machine pieced and machine quilted; 55 by 65 inches (139.7 by 165.1 cm).

For the past eight years, I have been creating quilts by "forming relationships" among patterned fabrics. In most cases, these relationships are the indistinct patterns created by arashi shibori. Often the piece begins with a fabric that has a particularly demanding "voice" that I try to add to as I orchestrate the interplay. The story of Icarus is spiritual and universal—it is about the value of striving upward, even if it is for the ultimately unattainable.

Jan Myers-Newbury
Pittsburgh, Pennsylvania

Circular Images No. 4
Fabric that has been hand dyed, discharged and dye painted; whole cloth construction, machine embroidered with polyneon thread, and machine quilted; 55 by 32 inches (139.7 by 81.3 cm).

My pieces range from boldly simple to intricate. In this

Bob Adams
Lafayette, Indiana

series, I used thread as a major element in the design of the pieces. The threads were applied entirely by free-motion machine stitching.

I Love a Mystery
Commercial and hand-dyed
cotton fabrics; machine
pieced and machine quilt-
ed; 58 by 50 inches (147.3
by 127 cm).

Sometimes I escape life's troublesome realities by retreating into my

studio and letting my hands, rather than my conscious mind, create a

Janet Steadman
Clinton, Washington

quilt. When this quilt was

done, I saw images that

brought back memories of an old 1940s radio show called *I Love a*

Mystery. It is easier for me to deal with the cleverness of a whodunit

mystery than the mysterious conundrums of the modern world.

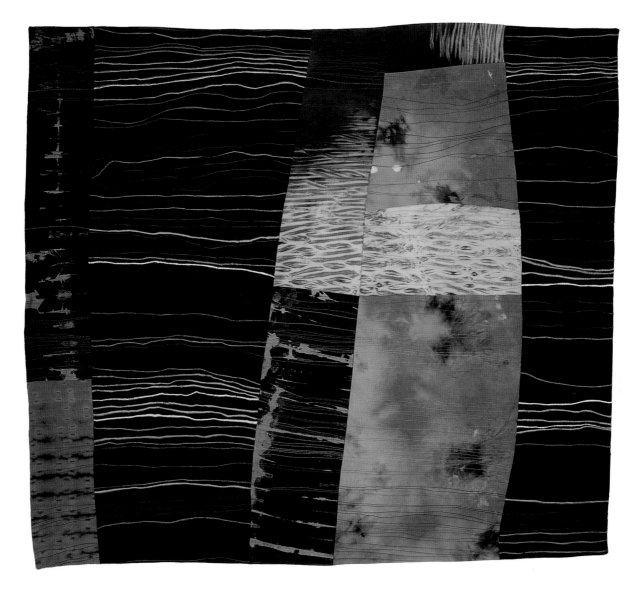

Elegant Legacy
Cotton and linen fabrics
that have been hand dyed
using a discharge process;
machine pieced, quilted
and embroidered; 44 by 40
inches (118 by 101.6 cm).

Elegant Legacy is the result of an exercise that I undertook to trust my intuitive ability as a visual artist. I had produced an ample supply of discharge-dyed fabrics with the hope of assembling pieces in an artful manner to highlight values and textures. After studying the resulting composition, I feel certain that, through me, my elegant female ancestors are showing their influence.

Barbara D. Cohen
Denver, Colorado

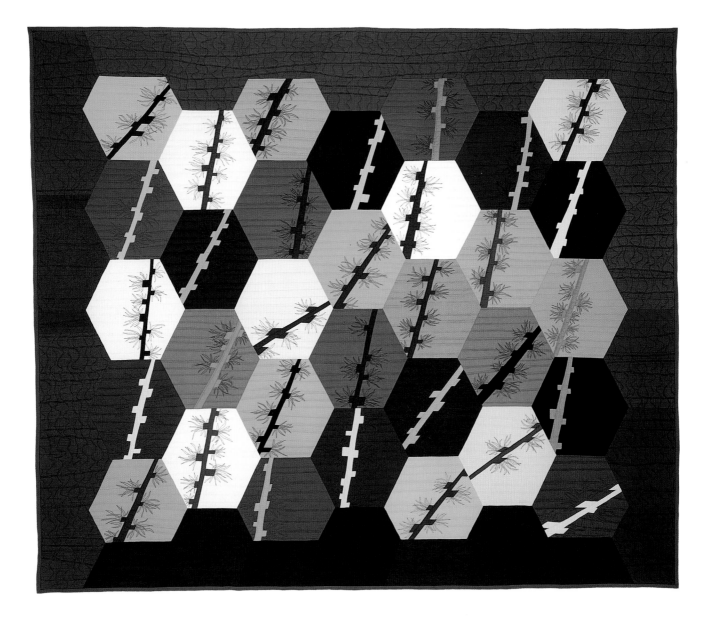

Larch in Spring
Cotton fabrics, pieced by improvisational and precision methods; machine quilted; 77 by 66 inches (195.6 by 167.6 cm).

A larch is a deciduous conifer. In fall, needles drop, leaving an irregular rhythm of nubs on each branch. In spring, needles burst forth in pom-poms, bathing

Heather Waldron Tewell
Anacortes, Washington

the tree in chartreuse. A friend, recognizing that I am inspired by incidental details from nature, brought me a larch branch from her hike in the woods. Not being able to get the bare branch out of my visual memory, I began to construct a quilt.

**Fragile Peace
of Mind**
Cotton fabrics; machine
pieced, appliquéd and
machine quilted; 55 by
56 inches (139.7 by
142.2 cm).

The calm, ordered white grid contrasts with the vibrating, lively strips
of colored fabric. The grid holds the vivid surface together, but at the

Cecile Trentini
Zurich, Switzerland

same time, the strips also surround and protect the frail

uncovered lines of cotton batting. These two elements interact and
create a fragile balance. The overall impression may be one of peace,
but how long will it last?

**CATHY RASMUSSEN EMERGING ARTIST AWARD SPONSORED BY
STUDIO ART QUILT ASSOCIATES**

Corporate Attire
Silk ties and other silk fabrics; machine pieced and machine quilted; 46 by 62 inches (116.8 by 157.5 cm).

The impetus for this quilt was my husband's decision to discard a number of silk ties after he had cleaned out his closet. These ties with their rich colors, wonderful textures, and intricate designs just begged to be used. This quilt flows from a single square into a design-as-you-go quilt that plays with color, texture, value, and shape.

Dale Fleming
Walnut Creek, California

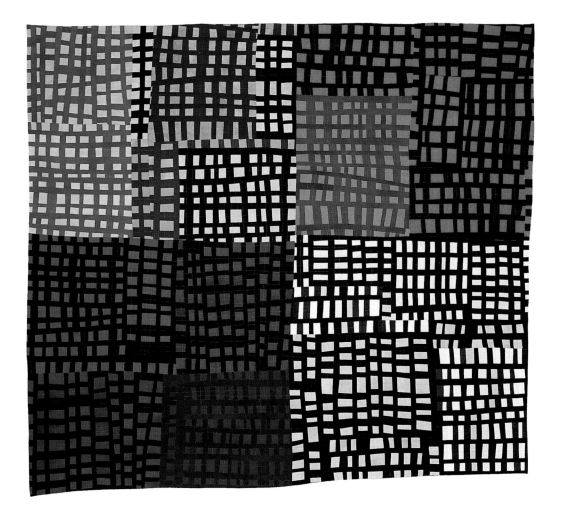

Constructions #33
Hand-dyed cotton fabric;
machine pieced and hand
quilted; 65 by 60 inches
(165.1 by 152.4 cm).

I have made 40 quilts for a series called *Constructions*. All of
them have been influenced by the renovation of a huge timber-

Nancy Crow
Baltimore, Ohio

frame barn built in 1884. The
proportions of the interior tim-
bers and boards are so exquisite that I am energized to work
intuitively to capture their dynamic proportions.

Within/Without 6
Cotton fabrics treated with shibori and other mechanical resist patterning techniques; machine pieced and machine quilted; 70 by 49 inches (177.8 by 124.5 cm).

In 1993, my husband and I moved to a classic 1950s home with walls of glass on the front that look out to a courtyard enclosed by a

Liz Axford
Houston, Texas

curved and perforated block wall. *Within/Without 6* depicts the wall at its most dramatic—backlit by the setting sun near the time of the summer solstice.

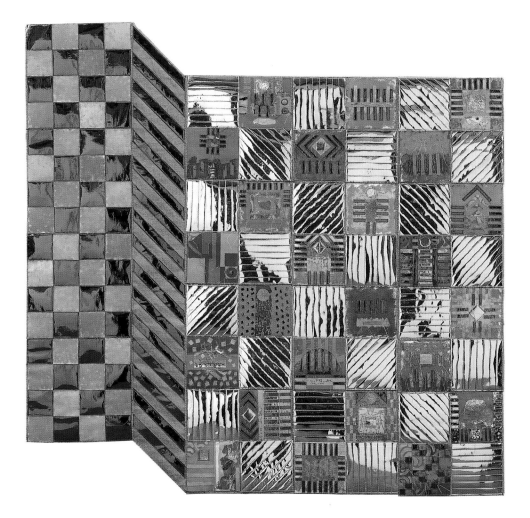

Checkpoint
Linen and cotton canvas, mylar, paint, found materials; machine-sewn appliqué collage, screen printing, hand-sewn construction. 54 by 54 inches (137.2 by 137.2 cm).

My work is inspired by textiles that are used in ritual and celebration as architectural embellishment, vesture, or ceremonial accessories. Geometric patterning, pieced construction, collage, and appliquéd mylar provide an expressive vocabulary as well as a means of solving formal problems. The inclusion of found and ready-made elements, as well as images from popular culture, encodes the work with contemporary references. The use of mylar, which responds to ambient light, adds to overall complexity of the surface.

Patricia Malarcher
Englewood, New Jersey

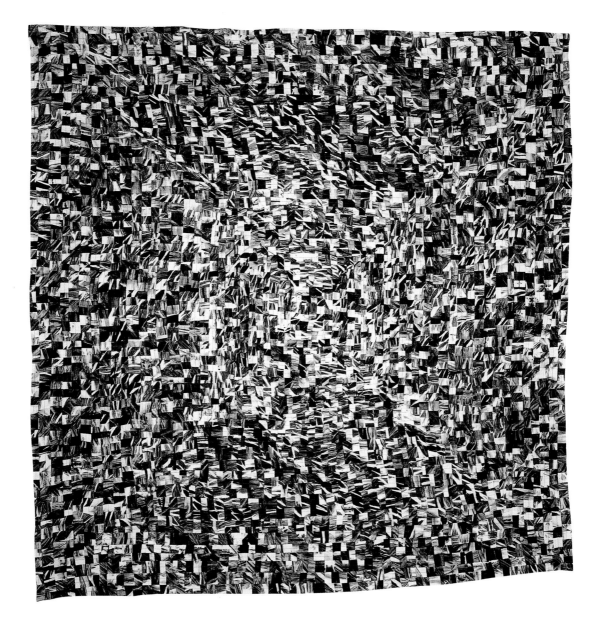

Redeye
Discharged shibori and discharged overdyed shibori cotton fabrics; machine pieced and machine quilted; 74 by 76 inches (188 by 193 cm).

I love transforming raw materials into objects of beauty and contemplation. I alter cloth through the processes of discharging, dyeing, cutting, pressing, and stitching. At some point, the materials

Phil D. Jones
Topeka, Kansas

come together to form something greater than the sum of the pieces. At that moment, I ask myself: Is this what I imagined? Does it embody the spirit and energy I envisioned? Did I get out of the way and allow this work to bloom? This is how the process works for me.

Fences in the Dunes

Cotton fabrics (some hand printed in the Caribbean Andros Islands); machine pieced, appliquéd, and quilted; 51 by 35 inches (129.5 by 88.9 cm).

All of my quilts reflect my loves and interests from both the past and the present. Sometimes they express my feelings of delight in surroundings, as does this quilt. I love the look of retaining fences along our local beaches that have been bent by ocean winds. I am fascinated by the straight lines of the wooden posts against undulating sand dunes that signal the interaction of man and nature.

Beatriz Grayson
Winchester, Massachusetts

This piece was inspired by the first time I saw pineapples growing in Maravu in Fiji. My work is influenced by the landscape and

Elizabeth Brimelow
Macclesfield, Cheshire, England

man's mark on it. I am interested in the marks that are made in the process of plowing, planting, and harvesting as well as the history that has shaped fields, woods, paths, and open spaces. Through my hands, I have a story to tell, and this connects me to other times, places, and cultures.

Maravu

Silk fabrics that have been direct and reverse appliquéd; hand and machine stitched, hand tied; 60 by 60 inches (152.4 by 152.4 cm). (Front view on page 60, reverse view on page 61.)

Perspective
Hand-painted cotton and silk organza; machine pieced, hand appliquéd, machine and hand quilted; 38 by 59 inches (96.5 by 149.9 cm).

My return to recognizable tree imagery reflects my interest in both the inner and outer selves and the ensuing dialogue between the two.

Erika Carter
Bellevue, Washington

Perspective symbolizes how differently two people can view the same subject with similarities and differences in perspective.

Floating 1
Rayon and cotton fabrics patterned with fiber-reactive dyes and block prints; whole cloth construction, hand quilted; 56 by 44 inches (142.2 by 111.8 cm).

My work conveys the primitive feelings evoked by my inner world. These feelings then transform into inspiration for the structures in my

Hui-Ling Yu
San Diego, California

work. These include leaves, cocoons, and seed pods. My imagery evolves primarily from nature. Personal emotion is combined with a study of the relationships among colors and shapes.

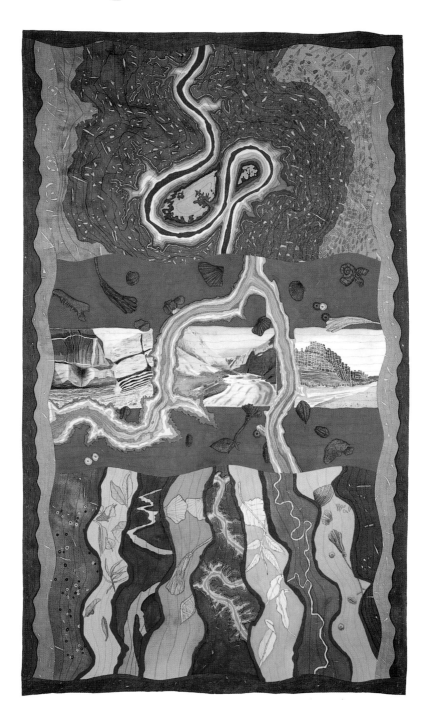

Current
Hand-painted fabric;
machine pieced and
machine quilted; 29
by 50 inches (73.7 by
127 cm).

This quilt was inspired by a rafting trip on the Colorado River through
Canyonlands National Park in Utah and a hiking trip in the Grand Canyon.

Donna June Katz
Chicago, Illinois

Another source of inspiration
was a gift from a friend—a

piece of rock from Utah containing bright orange fossilized shells. The quilt
reflects my interest in landscape, nature, geology, maps, patterning, a sense
of place and searching, and the restorative powers of nature and art.

Libby Lehman
Houston, Texas

Can anything be more beautiful than nature's designs? I have been fascinated lately with the shape of leaves—the flow of the curves, the endless color variations, and the unique individual shapes that imprint themselves on this quilt. *Windfall* is a tribute to Mother Nature in all her glory.

Windfall
Various fabrics, including hand-dyed and commercial cottons, organza, rayon, and metallic decorative threads; "potluck" appliqué, direct appliqué, bobbin drawing, machine embroidery, and machine quilting; 87 by 87 inches (221 by 221 cm).

BASS: In Your Dreams!
Hand-dyed and hand-painted cotton fabrics embellished with metallic fabric and threads as well as paint, foil, and ink; hand and machine pieced, hand appliquéd, and hand quilted; 86 by 79 inches (218.4 by 200.7 cm).

Nature's colors and patterns are the essence of my designs. My approach to quilt design is similar to a painter's—I use color, composition, and scale to capture the spirit of nature through the medium of textiles. Many classic works of art depict nature on a scale smaller than life, but I take life and amplify it. I believe that the greatest emotional and aesthetic impact of my works come from their larger-than-life scale.

Velda E. Newman
Nevada City, California

Broad Strokes
Cotton fabrics that have
been hand dyed, painted,
and printed with blocks
and screens; machine
pieced and machine quilt-
ed; 62 by 65 inches (157.5
by 165.1 cm).

Circular forms are fundamental to our universe—atoms and
plants, cells and bubbles, eyes and wheels. Circles often appear
to be perfect, such

Rosemary Hoffenberg
Wrentham, Massachusetts

as the earth or the

moon. *Broad Strokes* is my metaphor for this simple but
meaningful and complex shape.

**Reflections,
Burano, Italy,
Variation 1**
Hand-dyed and commercial
cotton fabrics; fused and
appliquéd, machine
stitched; 32 by 47 inches
(81.3 by 119.4 cm).

Over the years, I've taken a lot of photos in Italy, trying to capture the particular beauty of the light, color, and patterns that make it a special place for me. This quilt is one of a series of photos that I've tranformed into a tactile medium. I like the abstract nature of this photo quilt because you see the patterns created by the reflections first, and then you realize what the image is.

Barbara J. Schneider
McHenry, Illinois

**Byzantium X
(Strange
Attractors)**
Cotton fabrics; hand
pieced and hand quilted;
56 by 42 inches (142.2
by 106.7 cm).

In this work and the others in my *Byzantium Series*, I explore the arch—
an intriguing architectural form that appears to flirt with the

Marilyn Henrion
New York, New York

ambiguities of two- and three-
dimensional space. Inspired by
Byzantium architecture, the arch is also symbolic of the passageway
created as we exit one millennium and enter another.

The following passage from Alfred Lord Tennyson's poem *Ulysses* pro-
vides the viewer with a clue to my inspiration and intent in this series:

I am part of all that I have met,

Yet all experience is an arch

Wherethrough gleams that untravelled world.

Daily, I see around me, a myriad of untold stories waiting to be heard—

Old stone walls, broken fences, and abandoned barns.

They are the silent reminders of the fragile and complex relationship

between man and nature.

Denise Linet
Center Harbor, New Hampshire

Man struggles to tame and control.

Nature is patient and, in time—

Walls, fallen, are covered with ivy,

Fence posts lean, with rusted wire askew,

Birds fly in and out of the gaping eyes

of an abandoned building.

Fingers of barbed wire wind gently around a young sapling

as time tightens its grip.

Untold Stories
Hand-dyed cotton fabrics (some with photo transfers); machine pieced, hand and machine quilted; 40 by 40 inches (101.6 by 101.6 cm).

This piece is one of a series seeking to evoke

Linda Levin
Wayland, Massachusetts

the excitement of the

changing seasons and

the very changeable New England weather.

Walking the Dogs/Summer
Cotton fabrics treated with dyes, oil pastels, and colored pencils; machine pieced, direct and reverse appliquéd, machine embroidered, and machine quilted; 64 by 49 inches (162.6 by 124.5 cm). On loan from a private collection.

Urban Sprawl II (In Memory of Sidney)
Cottons and blends (some of which have been hand painted and embellished with various yarns, threads, and found objects); machine pieced, machine and hand appliquéd, machine quilted; 68 by 55 inches (172.7 by 139.7 cm).

This piece is the second of a series of work in which I explore our relationship with nature. In South Florida, urban sprawl grows like an uncontrolled brush fire, leaving behind large concrete and asphalt-covered areas.

Maya Schöenberger
Miami, Florida

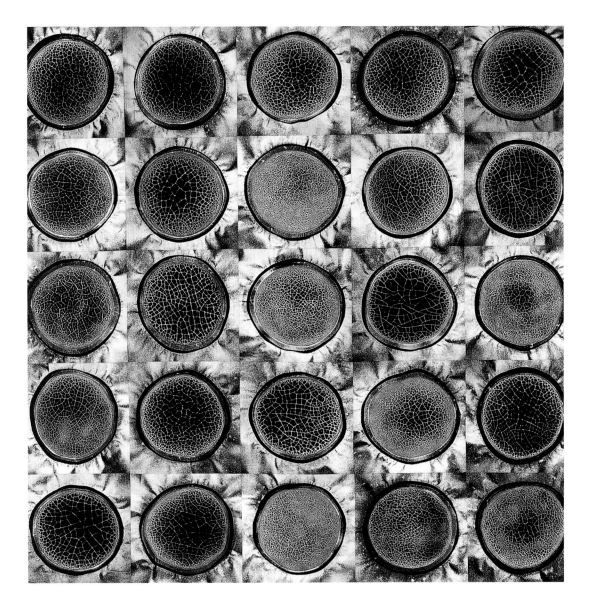

Illumination
100 percent cotton fabric
patterned with bleach and
potato dextrin starch resist;
machine pieced and
machine quilted; 62 by 62
inches (157.5 by 157.5 cm).

Our goal is for our works to have their own energy and presence. We achieve this by allowing the "sweet spot" (the perfect combination of

**Debra Lunn and
Michael Mrowka**
Lancaster, Ohio

process, fabric, and technique) to have its own voice. We are fascinated by the fractal marks created by our process and their dimensional quality, which imitates both the micro- and macrocosmic aspects of nature. The machine quilting is done to enhance the dimensional feeling of the image and to suggest living force fields.

We each have our own unique journey in life. We react to experiences and challenges in order to sculpt our characters and establish our values.

Lauren Rosenblum
Forest Hills, New York

Some journeys are treacherous, others are subtle. Our interpretation and reaction take us another step on our journey. Some welcome their lessons, others repel or avoid them due to fear or complacency. Regardless of the attempt at avoidance, the lessons will resurface and manifest themselves repeatedly, persisting and frustrating us.

Journey
Cotton fabric that has been patterned with fiber-reactive dyes, discharge paste, silk screens, and paint; machine pieced and hand quilted; 32 by 41 inches (81.3 by 104.1 cm).

Lost Mariner
100 percent cotton fabrics and cotton batting; machine pieced, paper pieced, hand appliquéd, machine quilted and hand beaded; 35 by 35 inches (88.9 by 88.9 cm).

This piece was the result of a challenge to use a certain fabric. I didn't care for the fabric, so it became a challenge to make something that I liked from it. I feel confined with preplanning a piece, so I planned only the mariner's compasses. The rest of the design was a result of what the piece called for. I ended up using the "challenge fabric" to frame the piece.

Ann Reed
Withamsville, Ohio

The title of this work comes from a poem entitled *Negative Hands* by Marguerite Duras, a French

Anne Woringer
Paris, France

novelist and film producer.

In the poem, Duras refers to the open-hand prints made by primitive people on the walls of archaeological sites

Les Mains Négatives
Linen from the nineteenth century that has been hand dyed and fused; machine appliquéd and machine quilted; 56 by 50 inches (142.2 by 127 cm).

JUROR'S AWARD OF MERIT

***Harbingers of
Spring***
Cotton fabrics that have
been hand dyed with indigo
through shibori techniques
of pole wrapping, stitching,
and pleating; hand and
machine pieced, hand
appliquéd, hand quilted;
23 by 51 inches (58.4 by
129.5 cm).

My work focuses on landscape art and textile techniques found in
Eastern and Western traditions. American quilting and Japanese shibori

Carol Anne Grotrian
Cambridge, Massachusetts

techniques are joined to create

the quiet stream surrounded by

New England pussy willows and Asian plum blossoms.

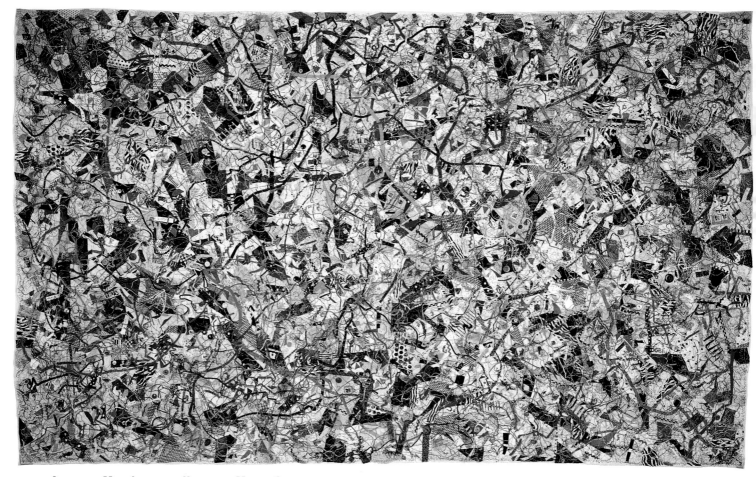

AWARD FOR MOST INNOVATIVE USE OF THE MEDIUM SPONSORED BY FRIENDS OF FIBER ART INTERNATIONAL

Revisiting Jackson
Hand-dyed and commercial fabrics embellished with a variety of materials, including buttons, cording, rickrack, lace, coins, stamps, paper clips, safety pins, candy wrappers, toys, and other found objects; fused and machine appliquéd, stapled and machine quilted; 104 by 65 inches (264.2 by 165.1 cm).

I have created a series of fiber-fragment quilts by working in a fairly random and spontaneous manner. I'm constantly reminded of the simple beauty of found objects, recycled materials, and castoffs.

Pat Kroth
Verona, Wisconsin

From my background in abstract painting, I recently remembered how much I enjoy Jackson Pollock's work. Now I feel as though I'm truly painting with fabric and thread.

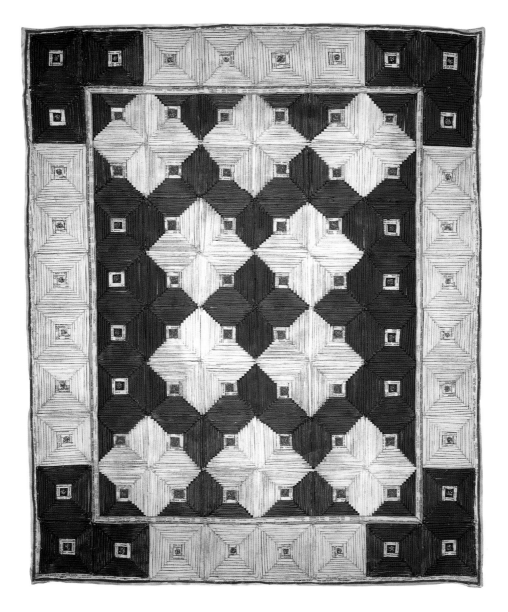

Twist Tied Log Cabin

3,500+ twist ties hand colored on each edge; cross-stitched into 80 log cabin squares, beaded in center, and assembled for the face layer; 34 by 41 inches (86.4 by 104.1 cm).

I spend hours making order from scraps and disposable artifacts. This work process is a ritual folly that distances the pace and transforms the waste of modern life. This piece pays homage to the traditional domestic arts, and it, as well as life, should be viewed with humor.

Amy Orr
Philadelphia, Pennsylvania

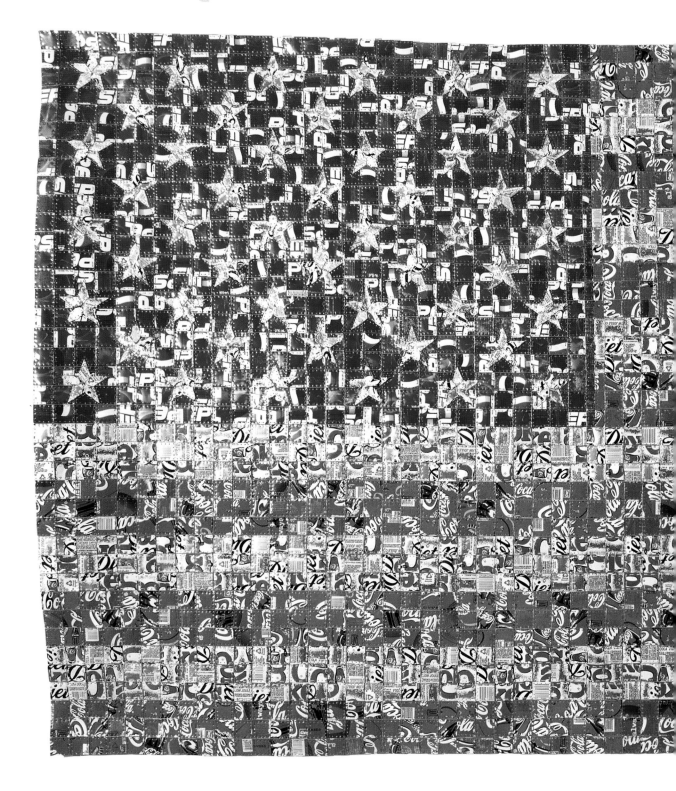

We live in a time of global influences, where huge corporations have worldwide profiles. We are seeing an Americanization of other cultures through the products these corporations produce. By

Janie Matthews
Darlington, Australia

recycling product packaging in a traditional quilt format, I have aimed to create work which has some evidence of the time, effort, and value of something made by hand in the face of runaway consumerism.

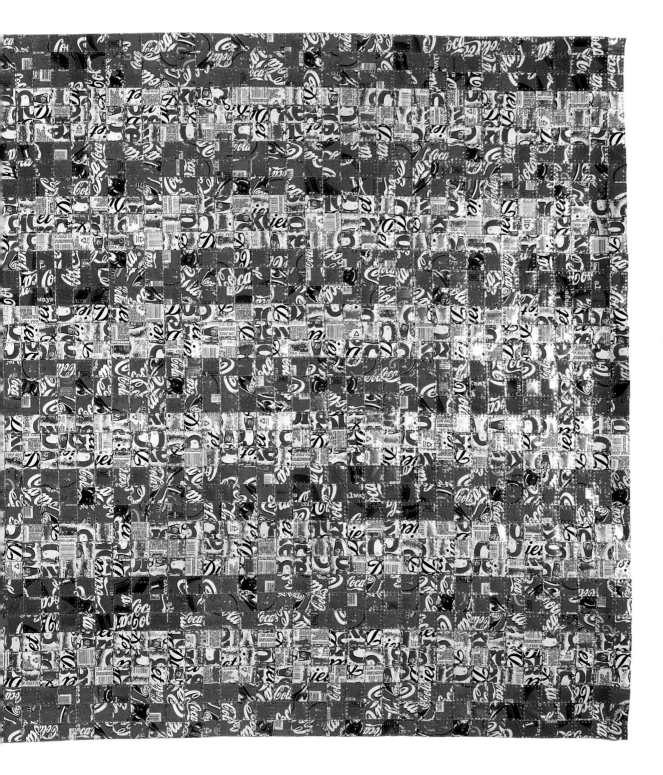

American Icon
Cotton fabric with recycled
aluminum soda cans; hand
appliquéd and hand quilt-
ed; 86 by 45 inches (218.4
by 114.3 cm).

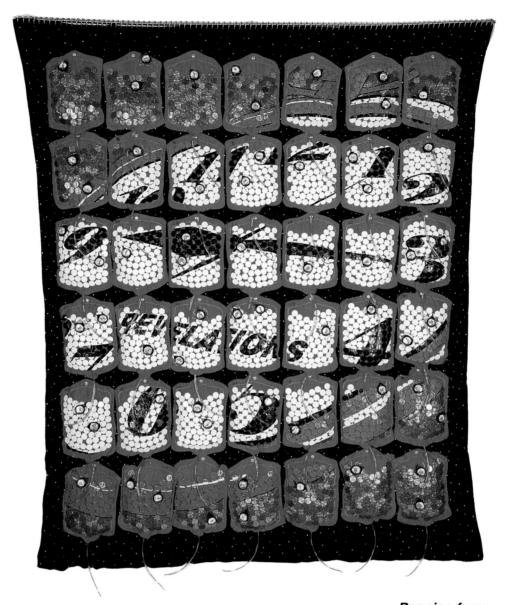

Pennies from Heaven/Make Your Ticks Count

Various fabrics and found objects, including pennies, velvet, satin, mesh, glass beads, clear plastic tubing, toy watches, copper wire; hand and machine stitched, hand painted; 58 by 69 inches (147.3 by 175.3 cm).

"Time is the coin of your life. It is the only coin you have, and only you can determine how it will be spent. Be careful lest you let other people spend it for you."

—Carl Sandburg

John w. Lefelhocz
Athens, Ohio

Is it time for a change?

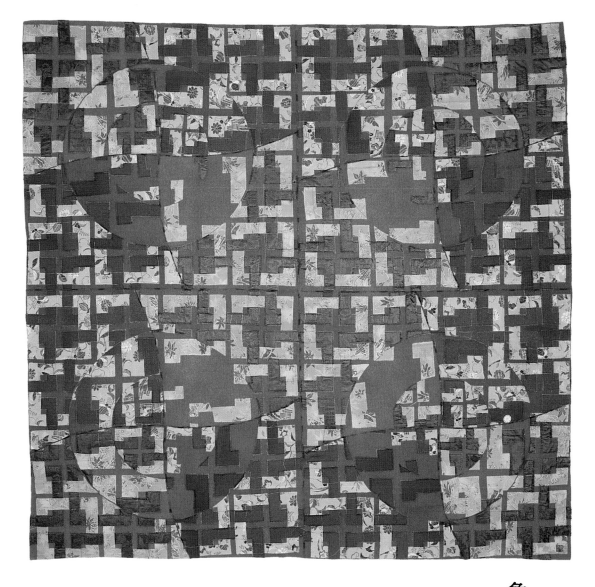

Syo #2 象
Antique silk fabric; machine pieced and machine appliquéd; 63 by 63 inches (106 by 106 cm).

This work was inspired by a particular piece of antique silk fabric. After I decided on the design that I wanted to use, I began the pleasant process of arranging the pieces. In the future, I would like to continue making quilts by refining the simplest patterns to create visually appealing works for my audience.

Harue Konishi
Tokyo, Japan

Sengakuji Temple Gables
Hand-dyed and cyanotype printed cottons; machine pieced and quilted; 44 by 44 inches (118 by 118 cm).

This piece was inspired by a couple of early morning walks around the Sengakuji Temple in Tokyo during the time I spent there in 1998 as a Fulbright memorial scholar. The strong color and design express my responses to the intensity of the light, time, and season there.

Tafi Brown
Alstead, New Hampshire

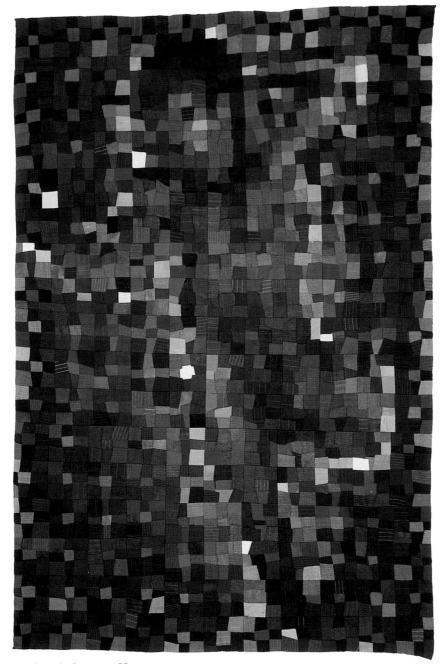

JUROR'S AWARD OF MERIT

Workman's Quilt
Overdyed men's suiting material; machine pieced and appliquéd, hand tied; 52 by 82 inches (132.1 by 208.3 cm).

Because my work is about memory and loss, I like to impose a sense of a real history, use, and wear on my materials. Up close, this image loses its clarity, and one sees that the "distant perfection" is actually flawed. As memories fade, the "repairs" serve to capture a moment and preserve it. The roughness of the holes and repaired frayed edges are intended as a visual marker for the essence of time. They are an attempt to retain an emotion associated with the past.

Scott Allen Ellegood
San Francisco, California

The figures in this piece are pictograms—symbols that suggest ideas, sensations, or states of being—created as similar, interchangeable units to suggest the mobility of memories. As each of us assembles and edits life's narrative, we create a sub-jective emotional cinema through which we continually reinterpret and redefine ourselves. *Figures 8* portrays a visual slice of this process of translating being into recollecting and experiencing into knowing.

Katherine K. Allen
Ft. Lauderdale, Florida

Figures 8
Commercial cottons and
painted cotton, silk and raw
canvas; machine appliquéd,
embroidered, and quilted;
60 by 38 inches (152.4 by
96.5 cm).

Middle Matzah
Silk screened and embroidered commercial cotton; whole cloth construction, hand quilted; 40 by 35 inches (101.6 by 88.9 cm).

Each spring, Jews celebrate the holiday of Passover with a traditional seder meal. At the seder we remember the time that Jews were enslaved in Egypt.

Louise Silk and Leslie A. Golomb
Pittsburgh, Pennsylvania

During the seder and the eight days of Passover, we eat matzah, a traditional flat bread. The matzah reminds us that the Jews left Egypt so quickly that their bread didn't have enough time to rise. This quilt, printed on matzah-like fabric, confronts the question asked by the youngest person at the seder table: "Why is this night different from all other nights?" The answer is our quest to understand the issues of race and bondage.

A Break from the Storm

Commercial cottons; machine appliquéd, embroidered, and quilted; 70 by 41 inches (177.8 by 104.1 cm).

I have been working on a series of images that deal with emotions within the family. The challenges and difficulties that can surround

Lori Lupe Pelish
Niskayuna, New York

even a young child's life can be overwhelming. This theme is explored in this piece. The mother and son are caught in a moment of time. They have turned their backs on the storm, while ignoring the debris, to experience a moment of pure joy.

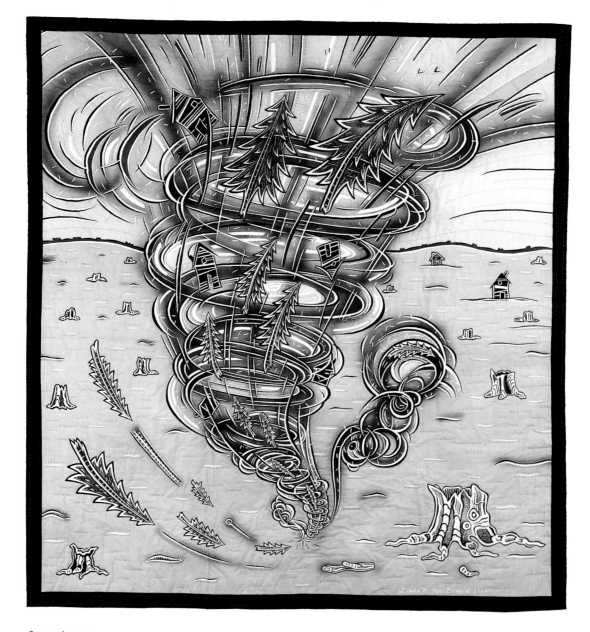

QUILTS JAPAN PRIZE

Into the Tornado
Cotton broadcloth that has been dyed, airbrushed, and brush painted with fiber-reactive dyes; whole cloth construction, hand quilted; 44 by 48 inches (111.8 by 121.9 cm).

I'm working on a series of quilts and drawings concerning what happens to trees—in northern California, it is quite an issue because they are disappearing. Do they dance away, fly, burn up, travel to Europe, or what? These trees have gone up through the funnel in a rare California tornado.

Linda MacDonald
Willits, California

Contour Highway
Cotton and rayon; machine
quilted; 56 by 41 inches
(142.2 by 104.1 cm).

This composition of images was created in the state between sleep
and awareness. The subdued appearance of the work symbolizes the

**Inge Mardal and
Steen Hougs**
Brussels, Belgium

materials of which dreams
are made, whereas the
busy and strangely popu-
lated motif reflects the day that lies ahead.

Time Piece: Millennium
Commercial and hand-dyed cotton patterned with ink, computer-generated images, paint, and found objects; pieced and appliquéd with hand and machine stitches, machine quilted; 33 by 38 inches (83.8 by 96.5 cm).

This piece is a part of a series of five time-related works: *Nonce, Dusk, Monday, Summer,* and finally, this grand measure of time, *Millennium*—the stroke of midnight when the old milliennium changes to the new.

Gerry Chase
Seattle, Washington

DOMINI MCCARTHY MEMORIAL AWARD

This is the third in a series of quilts inspired by a 1996 trip to Russia. Much residue, both physical and figurative, remains after the fall of communism. A quote from David K. Shipler's book *Russia: Broken Idols, Solemn Dreams* plays out across ripped wall posters on the crumbling facades, contrasting the party line of a social realist cityscape with the rich interior lives of its inhabitants.

Robin Schwalb
Brooklyn, New York

Heroic Optimism
Photo-silk screened, stenciled, overdyed, and commercially available cotton fabrics; painted polyester, machine pieced; hand appliquéd and reverse appliquéd, hand quilted; 60 by 82 inches (152.4 by 208.3 cm).

**All Dressed Up
with No Place
to Go**
Commercial cottons, tulle;
machine pieced, appliquéd,
embroidered and quilted;
67 by 47 inches (170.2 by
119.4 cm).

This piece is part of a series of work based on photographs that I took in Santa Fe, New Mexico, and the south of France. These two

Marcia Stein
San Francisco, California

lovely Provencal ladies would no doubt prefer a night on the town to being cooped up in a shop window—but such is the life of a French mannequin.

Wine with Lichtenstein
Commercial and hand-dyed cottons (some of which have been painted, airbrushed and discharged with potato dextrin resist); machine pieced, appliquéd, embroidered and quilted; 42 by 62 inches (106.7 by 157.5 cm).

This piece could be subtitled "a toast to the new millennium." Since all human endeavors build on what has gone before, this quilt references the history of Western art: the Greek column; still life; cubism and Picasso; Roy Lichtenstein and the Pop Art Movement. It was made in honor of the quilt artists of the new millenium—something on which to build.

Miriam Nathan-Roberts
Berkeley, California

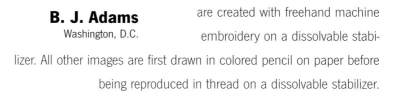

JUROR'S AWARD OF MERIT

Nature's color studio works overtime, reflecting the seasons. Work done in my studio tends to duplicate this bounty of colors. The trees in this piece

B. J. Adams
Washington, D.C.

are created with freehand machine embroidery on a dissolvable stabilizer. All other images are first drawn in colored pencil on paper before being reproduced in thread on a dissolvable stabilizer.

A Seasonal Spectrum

Painted canvas and dupioni silk; machine pieced, appliquéd, and embroidered; 56 by 21 inches (142.3 by 53.4 cm).

The Sower
Commercial fabrics, yarn, and beads; hand and machine pieced, direct and reverse appliquéd, fused, hand embroidered, hand and machine quilted; 62 by 83 inches (157.5 by 210.8 cm).

This piece is part of a series about the women in my family. The images are derived from a combination of history/myth and personal memory.

Denise Burge
Cincinnati, Ohio

Sometimes the woman in this series appears as storyteller, at other times she presents herself through the metaphor of a tree or mountain. In *The Sower*, my grandmother appears as a blue jay wearing pink panties—a fierce bird with a strident, passionate call. She was a woman who half-resided in her garden, wresting vegetation from the sun-dried red clay of North Carolina.

The Cookbook/Hierophant: Card #5 in the Kitchen Tarot

Cotton duck canvas and other cotton fabrics embellished with airbrush paint and found objects (including embroidery floss, buttons, glass bugle beads, ceramic alphabet beads, antique leaded glass beads, antique rhinestone beads, thimble, and a scissors trinket); hand and machine embroidered, hand quilted; 71 by 61 inches (180.3 by 154.9 cm).

This is the fifth in a series of Kitchen Tarot quilts that began in 1998 with The Colander/Fool: #0. We've got 72 quilts to go! This quilt represents the tarot deck's authority figure, high priest, or pope. In the Turtle Moon Test Kitchen, we look at the cookbook, and then go wild with our creations!

Susan Shie and James Acord
Wooster, Ohio

Temptress with a Teapot

Painted and sanded canvas, screen printing, and mixed media including vintage tablecloth, color laser transfer and inkjet photo transfers, photocopy fabric, horsehair netting, couching with gold braid, beads, and sequins; bound with beads, machine quilted with monofilament; 40 by 70 inches (101.6 by 177.8 cm).

Who wouldn't be tempted to attend a tea party with a voluptuous blonde Venus pouring the tea?

Wendy Huhn
Dexter, Oregon

Paper Plates and Bone China, Some Hand Painted

Various fabrics, paper, paint, beads, buttons, silver leaf, cloth with photocopy transfers, and found objects including vintage Dresden plate pieces, a glove, paper fortunes; machine and hand pieced, hand appliquéd, hand quilted and tied; 52 by 41 inches (132.1 by 104.1 cm).

Combining various materials and textures is one of my favorite parts of making quilts. Vintage quilt pieces, an artist's canvas painted and stenciled with black and white acrylic paint, and a ragged handmade paper inspired this quilt.

Jane Burch Cochran
Rabbit Hash, Kentucky

The title came to me, and I continued a play with words in the piece. Chinese fortunes from cookies were transferred to cloth and then zigzag stitched to the plate. "Bone" was the last word that came to me, so serving dog biscuits seemed appropriate. I added silver leaf to a commercial fabric to complete the setting.

**TV Test Pattern:
The Center of
Chaos**
Commercial and hand-dyed
cotton fabrics that have
been airbrushed,
appliquéd, fused, embroi-
dered, and beaded by hand
and machine; machine
quilted; 52 by 52 inches
(132 by 132 cm).

Here's how to get started in mosaic artwork: Begin with a cat (such
as mine) with a serious yen for flowers. Throw some blooms in your
favorite vase and set them in

Cheri Arnold
Columbus, Ohio

your newest hiding place. (You
know, the one you're sure she won't be able to sniff out this time.)
Clearly, you're in denial...but the good news is that you can use all
that busted glass and pottery as inspiration for a magnificent mosaic
cat memorial such as this one!

The Kissss (From the MOM Series)
Cotton broadcloth patterned with paste resist and dyes; whole cloth construction, machine quilted; 16 by 22 inches (40.6 by 55.9 cm).

The first work in my *MOM* series, called *Don't Tread on MOM*, opened a wellspring of ideas for autobiographical quilts that is gushing faster than I can translate them into quilts. The snakes in these pieces are covered with flowers, birthstones, and favorite things that symbolize family members. Other objects refer to the theme or title of the quilt. I allow the skin patterns on the snakes to develop spontaneously and am often surprised by their unplanned meanings.

Marilyn L. Harrison
Boca Raton, Florida

  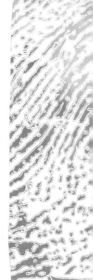

I made this set of five fingerprints on fabric using the palette of colors left from painting a picture. They explore the many differences in

Barbara W. Watler
Hollywood, Florida

graphic design along with those created by genetics, age, life experience, and vocation. The use of color along with the freedom of painting was great fun after using only black and white in 20 fingerprint quilts that began this series.

Painter's Prints
Cotton fabric that has been
hand painted with perma-
nent silk dyes; reverse
appliquéd and machine
quilted; 77 by 15 inches
(195.6 by 38.1 cm).

A High Fiber Tea
Various materials including cotton, silk, velour, lamé, satin, beads, paint, and found objects; hand embroidered, pieced, appliquéd, and beaded; machine pieced, appliquéd, couched, and quilted; 34 by 48 inches (86.4 by 122 cm).

Out of nowhere I had a desire to create a three-dimensional teapot pouring into a free-floating cup. It only seemed proper to place it against a 1950s background and surround it with foods tied together with a braided vine. I like to tell people that it's a "diet" quilt—one that is high in fiber and low in calories!

Kathy Davie
Denver, Colorado

Marie Wohadlo
Chicago, Illinois

OVER-adjust-advertise-all-amplify-analyze-assess-bill-burden-caffeinate-cast-commit-complicate-concern-consume-correct-cultivate-diversifydrive-due-eager-educate-emphasize-estimate-excite-exert-extend-flow-focus-govern-haul-hype-inflate-inform-load-look-night-orchestrate-mediate-pass-pressure-privilege-process-promise-reach-react-refine-regulate-rely-see-sell-sensitize-sophisticate-spend-simulate-stress-strewn-suspicious-take-tax-think-tired-use-whelm-work-wrought.

W.O.W. (Weight of the World)
Silk and cotton fabrics stitched with polyester thread and treated with my own "secret" imaging processes; machine embroidery and machine quilting; 36 by 48 inches (91.4 by 121.9 cm).

King of Cups
Hand-dyed cotton and variegated rayon thread; fused appliqué and free-motion machine quilting; 57 by 72 inches (144.8 by 182.9 cm).

This quilt is named after the tarot card called the "king of cups," and there are 14 vessels or cups in this quilt. I love ambiguity: Is the central image an orange with a handle or a teacup with a slice of orange? I hope the viewer has as much fun looking at it as I did making it.

Robbi Joy Eklow
Grayslake, Illinois

The Dairy Barn Southeastern Ohio Cultural Arts Center is a unique arts facility in the Appalachian foothills. Its year-round calendar of events features both juried and curated exhibitions of work by regional, national, and international artists. In addition, the facility is the venue for festivals, performances, and a full range of classes for children and adults.

ABOUT THE DAIRY BARN

The history of the Dairy Barn is as colorful as its exhibits. Built in 1913, the structure housed an active dairy herd until the late 1960s. After sitting idle about 10 years, the building was scheduled for demolition. Fortunately, local artist Harriet Anderson and her husband, Ora, recognized the building's potential as a much needed regional arts center. They worked tirelessly to rally community support to save the dilapidated structure. With only nine days to spare, the demolition order was reversed, and the building was placed on the National Register of Historic Places. The Dairy Barn Southeastern Ohio Cultural Arts Center, a nonprofit organization, was born.

The architects retained the original character of the building through several renovation projects as it evolved from a seasonal, makeshift exhibit space into a first-class, fully accessible arts facility. Early 2001 saw the completion of a one million dollar renovation project. The ground level now houses a 6,600-square-foot exhibition space and a 400-square-foot retail gift shop that features work by regional and exhibiting artists. The formerly unused 7,000-square-foot upper level haymow now includes two large classroom spaces; three large multipurpose rooms suitable for classes, performances, and special events; offices for the staff; and storage space.

The Dairy Barn is supported by admissions, memberships, corporate sponsorships, grants, and donations. The staff is assisted by a large corps of volunteers who annually donate thousands of hours of time and talent. For a calendar of events and information about other Dairy Barn programs, contact the Dairy Barn Cultural Arts Center, P.O. Box 747, Athens, Ohio 45701, USA; phone, 740-592-4981; or visit the Internet site, www.dairybarn.org.

Previous **Quilt National** installations.

The complete Quilt National '01 collection will be on display from May 26 through September 2, 2001, at the Dairy Barn Southeastern Ohio Cultural Arts Center located at 8000 Dairy Lane in Athens, Ohio. Three separate groups of Quilt National '01 works (identified as Collections A, B, and C) will then begin a two-year tour of museums and galleries. Host venues will display only a portion of the full Quilt National '01 collection.

SHOW ITINERARY

Tentative dates and locations are listed below. **It is recommended that you verify this information by contacting a specific host venue prior to visiting the site.**

For an updated itinerary, or to receive additional information about hosting a Quilt National touring collection, contact the Dairy Barn Cultural Arts Center at P.O. Box 747, Athens, Ohio, 45701; phone: 740-592-4981; e-mail: info@dairybarn.org; or consult our Internet site at www.dairybarn.org.

5/26 - 9/3/01	Athens, Ohio; Dairy Barn Cultural Arts Center [full collection]
10/1 - 11/30/01	St Louis, Missouri; The City Museum [A, B, & C]
12/4/01 - 2/17/02	Sacramento, California; Crocker Museum of Art [C]
2/2 - 4/07/2002	Huntington, West Virginia; Huntington Museum of Art [A & B]
4/4 - 4/7/2002	Lancaster, Pennsylvania; Quilters' Heritage Celebration [C]
9/8 - 10/20/2002	Bloomingdale, Illinois; Bloomingdale Park District Museum [B]
11/7/02 - 2/10/03	Columbus, Ohio; Riffe Gallery [C]
4/3 - 4/6/03	Lancaster, Pennsylvania; Quilters' Heritage Celebration [A & B]
10/3 - 11/25/03	Laurel, Mississippi; Lauren Rogers Museum of Art [A]